FIRST Rhymes

For John Richard Piggy,
champion comforter and scrambled-egg maker,
and for
Archibald Charles
who asked for still more mamma songs.
With all my love and a million hugs to you both.

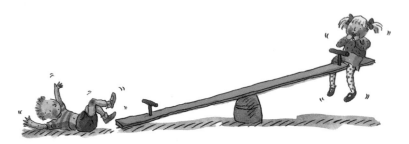

ORCHARD BOOKS
96 Leonard Street, London EC2A 4RH
Orchard Books Australia
14 Mars Road, Lane Cove, NSW 2066
1 85213 706 1
First published in Great Britain in 1994
Text copyright © Lucy Coats 1994
Illustrations copyright © Selina Young 1994
The right of Lucy Coats to be identified as the author and Selina Young as the illustrator of this work
has been asserted by them in accordance with the Copyright, Designs and Patents Act, 1988.
A CIP catalogue record for this book is available from the British Library.
Printed in Belgium

FIRST Rhymes

A Day of Rhymes, Games and Songs

LUCY COATS

Illustrated by SELINA YOUNG

ORCHARD BOOKS

CONTENTS

MORNINGS

AFTERNOONS

EVENINGS AND AFTER DARK

MORNINGS

WAKING UP AND BREAKFAST TIME

It's five in the morning,
I *know* it's not day.
But I am AWAKE
And I'm longing to play.
My toys are no fun
So I've thrown them all out.
I don't *think* my teddies
Will mind if I shout.
Oh! Look! It's my Mummy!
Oh! Hello! Here's Dad.
Oh! . . .
     Is getting up now so *terribly* bad?

Upsadaisy, little baby,
Draw the curtains wide.
Let the sun's fat smiley face
Come shining right inside.

Upsadaisy, little baby,
Jump out of your cot.
Watch the rain on the window pane
DRIPPITY SPLIT SPLAT SPLOT!

Fast asleep in Africa,
Waking up in France,
Getting up each morning
Is a time to sing and dance.

Waffles in the garden,
Fried eggs by the sea,
Cornflakes in the kitchen:
Smells like breakfast time to me.

Monday's Child chews kippered plaice,

Tuesday's Child has an eggy face.

Wednesday's Child is full of toast,

Thursday's Child can eat the most.

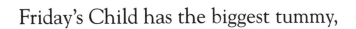

Friday's Child has the biggest tummy,

Saturday's Child throws beans at his mummy.

But the Child who is born on the Sabbath Day
Has sunlight for breakfast, with buttered sea-spray.

The doors on the car go clunk, clunk, slam
Clunk clunk slam, clunk clunk slam.
The doors on the car go clunk, clunk, slam
All day long.

The engine on the car goes cough, rattle, vrooom
Cough rattle vrooom, cough rattle vrooom.
The engine on the car goes cough, rattle, vrooom
All day long.

The tyres on the car go splat, zoom, splash
Splat zoom splash, splat zoom splash.
The tyres on the car go splat, zoom, splash
All day long.

The wipers on the car go swish, swish, squeak
Swish swish squeak, swish swish squeak.
The wipers on the car go swish, swish, squeak
All day long.

The shopping in the boot goes clink, clank, crash
Clink clank crash, clink clank crash.
The shopping in the boot goes clink, clank, crash
All day long.

The daddy at the wheel goes tootle, toot, parp
Tootle toot parp, tootle toot parp.
The daddy at the wheel goes tootle, toot, parp
All day long.

The children in the back go wiggle, squiggle, waaah
Wiggle squiggle waaah, wiggle squiggle waaah.
The children in the back go wiggle squiggle waaah
All day long.

The mummy in the front goes shout, yell, shush
Shout yell shush, shout yell shush.
The mummy in the front goes shout, yell, shush
All day long.

The family in the car get home at last
Home at last, home at last,
The family in the car get home at last
All Saturday long.

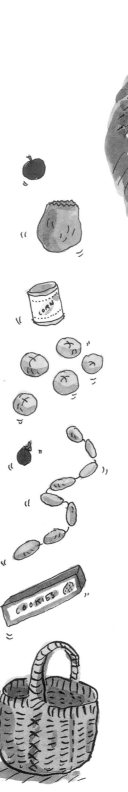

Eeny, Meeny, Miny, Mo,
Count the shoppers as they go.
Some have baskets, some have none,
Count the shoppers one by one.

Eeny, Meeny, Miny, Mo,
Count the buses as they go.
Some are empty, some are full,
And this one's coming home from school.

Goosey Goosey Gander,
This is where we wander,
Up and down the High Street
And left into the Baker.
There we saw a brown bun
With currants one, two, three,
So we put it in a paper bag
And took it home for tea.

HELPING

P owder, bubbles, splish splash sploshing,
Helping Mum to do the washing.
Wind must blow and sun must shine,
Hang the washing on the line.
Spray the dirt off, scrub the muck,
Helping Daddy clean his truck.
Peel the carrots, chop, chop, crunch,
Helping Mum to make the lunch.
Drying up goes clink clank clink,
Helping Daddy at the sink.
Dig my fork in, pull up weeds,
Helping Mum to sow her seeds.
Cheese and eggs and krispiepops,
Helping Daddy at the shops.
Tea and toast and milk and bread,
In the bath and off to bed.
Rain, or cloud or frosty weather,
We all like to help together.

Oranges and lemons,
Raisins and drop scones,
Eggs, milk and flour,
It'll take half-an-hour.
Heat knobs of butter
Till they spit, splat and splutter.
Ready or not?
Let's eat while they're hot!

Mary, Mary in January
How does your garden grow?
With snowdrop bells,
And spent snail shells,
And hungry birds all in a row.

Round and round the garden,
Like a squiggly worm,
Wriggle down my sister's neck,
Watch her squeal and squirm.

I had a little piece of earth,
Nothing would it grow
But a tangled crop of weeds,
Sunshine, rain or snow.

My granny and her sack of tools
Came to visit me,
So now I've got a bed of blooms
And one small apple tree.

SCHOOLTIME

A is for aeroplane

B is for bird

C is for clouds in the sky

D is for duckling

E is for egg

F is for feather and fly

G is for granny

H is for hugs

I is for "I love you too!"

J is for jellyfish

K is koala

L is for lions in the zoo

20

M is for marmalade

N is for nuts

O is for olives with stones

P is for palace

Q is for queen

R is for royal red thrones

S is for storms

T is for tempests

U is "Umbrellas up, please!"

V is for violin

  W is whistle

X is for xylophone keys

Y is for yellow and yoghurt
and yacht and yawns when
you've had a late night

Z is for zebra and zigzag
and zoom and zipping
your jacket up tight

One hungry baby
Two front teeth,
Three dribbly chins
With bibs underneath.
Four bubbly bathtimes
To wash off the crumbs.
Five sploshy splashers
Five wet Mums.
Six funny Dads
Drying six button noses,

Seven big sisters
Counting tails and toeses.
Eight fat teddies
Ready for bed.
Nine soft pillows
Nine sleepy heads.
Ten good babies
Tucked up tight,
Twenty tired parents
Waving Good Night.

red

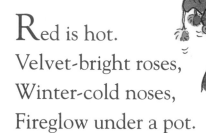

Red is hot.
Velvet-bright roses,
Winter-cold noses,
Fireglow under a pot.

Orange is sweet.
Juice in the morning,
Last sunset warning
Of daytime heat.

orange

pink

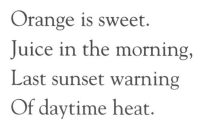

Pink is pleasant
Baby's first mittens,
Ribbons on kittens,
Bows on a present.

Purple is deep.
Far starlit spaces,
Shadows on faces,
Fast asleep.

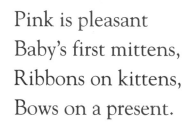

purple

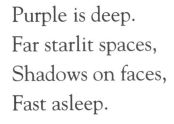

24

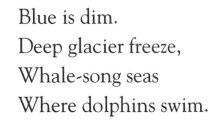

blue

Blue is dim.
Deep glacier freeze,
Whale-song seas
Where dolphins swim.

Green is bright.
Leaves in bud,
Grass from mud
Overnight.

green

yellow

Yellow is fun.
Bunched-up bananas,
Brave lemon banners
Blow in the sun.

Black is bold.
Stormy weather,
Raven feather
Dark as coal.

black

White is clean.
Blazing headlights,
Powdered snow fights,
Alpine scene.

white

Little old banger, big new bus,
Tea full tummy, hungry octopus,
Winter wet rain, dry summer sun,
Melty cold ice-cream, hot cross bun.
Top of the cupboard, dusty bottom shelf,
Old as Grandpa, young as yourself.
Soft fluffy feathers, hard stony rocks,
Clean white washing, dirty black socks.
Weak milky tea, strong shiny steel,
Square ironed handkerchief, round rolling wheel.
Red says "Stop!", green shouts "Go!"
"Yes!" means you can, you can't growls "No!"
Opening the window, shutting the door,
Get off the table, sit on the floor.
Short fat bollards, long thin lamp posts,
Sing "Happy Birthday!", whisper to sad ghosts.
Into the house, out of the car,
Day time light, night time star.
Autumn dead leaf, spring sprouting rose,
Find all the opposites under your nose!

Head at the top
Mango shape
Hair like a haystack
Mouth agape.
Eyes like almonds
Ears like shells
Nose points forward
Snuff sniffle smell.

Neck on shoulders
Broad as a bride
Arms and elbows
One each side.
Hands for clapping
Finger and thumb
Sitting down bottom
Big fat tum.

Legs all lanky
Long like masts
Knees all knobbly
Marching past.
Toes all tickly
Two flat feet
One little body
All complete.

"head"
"eyes"
"hair"
"nose"
"hand"
"ears"
"neck"
"mouth"
"shoulder"
"elbow"
"arm"
"tum"
"bottom"
"finger"
"thumb"
"knee"
"leg"
"toe"
"foot"

Bark little spotty dog,
Bark, bark, bark,
Run, run, woof,
In the street and the park.

Mew fluffy tabby cat,
Mew for your milk.
Purr when I tickle
Your tummy of silk.

Moo sleepy brown cow,
Moo at the gate.
Will Farmer milk you
Or will he be late?

Baa baby woolly sheep,
Bleat for your Mam.
Baa when you find her
Silly white lamb.

Neigh, neigh chestnut horse,
Mane and tail fly.
Gallop, gallop to the gate,
Tuck your hooves up high.

Cluck busy speckled hen,
Cluck, cluck, scratch.
Hurry, hurry to your nest,
Will the eggs hatch?

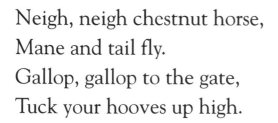

Quack yellow mother duck,
Quack for your brood.
Quick, quack over here,
Lots of lovely food.

Tweet, tweet, chirpy bird,
Singing in your tree.
Look out from the topmost branch,
Tell me what you see.

LUNCHTIME

Hickory, dickory, dock,
It must be one o'clock.
The mouse in my tum
Is beating his drum,
Tickety, tappety, tock.

Little Sue Horner
Sneaks round the corner
Munching salt crisps on the sly.
She won't eat her lunch
If she takes one more crunch
And her mum's baked a nice liver pie.

AFTERNOONS

TIRED TIMES AND NAPS

Cross Patch
Must not snatch
Go to your bed and rest.
Lie as still
As a mouse, until
It's time to get up and dressed.

Don't care was made to care,
Don't care wouldn't have done
If she'd gone for her nap,
Not played with the tap
And stuck out her little pink tongue.

January new beginning,
 Resolutions,
 Snowflakes spinning.

February frosty fogs,
 Winter shivers,
 Fire-warm logs.

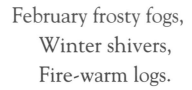

March blows windy, smells of spring,
 Leaves peek out,
 Brave blackbirds sing.

April showers fall soft and slow,
 Earth wakes up,
 And green things grow.

May Day ribbons round a pole,
 May-time babies,
 Lamb and foal.

June brings summer blazing in,
 Scent of roses,
 Sun on skin.

July joy means school is out,
    Time for picnics,
    Heat and drought.

August goes on holiday,
    Sandy castles,
    Friends to stay.

September sees the autumn come,
    Plough the fields
    One by one.

October gales lash the trees,
    Leaves a-swirling,
    Crashing seas.

November nights all crisp and cold,
    Winter coats
    For young and old.

December dark, yet full of light,
    Christmas carols,
    Star so bright.

Rain, rain, go away,
Sun come out so I can play.
Rain, rain, go and hide,
Let's have sunshine countrywide.

It's raining, it's pouring,
Staying indoors is boring.
I want to kersplosh
In my new mackintosh
And run off to Russia exploring.

The North Wind brings snow
So out we all go,
Me, Millie and Billy and Ben.
We'll skip through the storm
And keep ourselves warm
And take it in turns on the swing.
Playing,
And take it in turns on the swing.

Pink sky at night,
    Postman's delight.
Red sky in the morning,
    Milkman's warning.

OUTDOOR GAMES

Girls and boys come play in the park,
We're counting the animals into the ark.
I'll be a leopard and you be a lion
And let's all pretend that the monkey is Brian.
Up the ladder and down the slide,
Let's crawl on our Noah's ark side by side.
One and two and three and four,
In by the window and out by the door.
Five and six and seven and eight,
If the flood comes we'll all sink with the weight.
Nine and ten plus Noah and son,
Last one's a tortoise, so you'd better RUN!

Ring-a-ring o' roses
A roundabout of noses,
A-swisha, A-swisha,
We all whirl round.

See saw, Margery Daw,
Which one of us can go faster?
Whee! up and down,
Big bump on the ground,
And Johnny's knee needs a big plaster.

I met a lion in the park,
I took him home for tea,
But when I'd fed him bread and jam
He wouldn't play with me.

I met a camel in the rain,
We both got very wet,
But when I took him home to Mum,
He wouldn't be my pet.

I met a monkey in the street,
She had a baby, too,
But when I asked them home to lunch,
They went to Timbuctoo.

I met my Daddy at the shop,
He'd bought me a surprise.
It had a little curly tail,
And big brown puppy eyes.

Row, row, row your boat
Gently down the stream,
If you catch a jellyfish
Wave your arms and scream.

Row, row, row your boat
Gently round the lake,
Watch out for the crocodile
And look out for the snake.

Row, row, row your boat
Gently down the river,
If you see a polar bear
Don't forget to shiver.

Row, row, row your boat
Gently out to sea,
If you meet a big blue whale
Ask her home for tea.

41

Off to the sand,
Off to the sea,
Mummy and Daddy
And Teddy and Me.

Sun's very hot,
Cream on my nose,
Dance in the waves,
Dabble my toes.

Buckets and spades,
Castles and moats,
Seagulls and seashells
And bobbing bright boats.

Ice-creams all melting
And lollies to lick,
Frisbees to throw
And beachballs to kick.

Wide open yawns
And eyelids that drop,
Pack up the picnic
For home's the next stop.

INDOOR GAMES

Humpty Dumpty stood on his head,
Humpty Dumpty fell out of bed.
All his silk carpets
And all his soft mats
Couldn't stop Humpty from going *Kersplat!*

Ride a red bike to Galveston Dyke
To race a small boy on his rickety trike.
With jam on his fingers and mud on his nose
He shall spread laughter wherever he goes.

This little piggy flew to Luton
This little piggy sulked at home.
This little piggy crunched doughnuts
This little piggy ate crumbs.
And this little piggy cried, "Wee, wee wee!
I need nice new knickers, please, Mum!"

This is the way the bus driver drives,
Startspeedupstop, startspeedupstop.
This is the way the bus driver drives,
Startspeedupstartspeedupstop.

This is the way the train driver drives,
Rattlediglide, rattlediglide.
This is the way the train driver drives,
Rattledirattlediglide.

This is the way the car driver drives,
Honketyswerve, honketyswerve.
This is the way the car driver drives,
Honketyswerve, honketyswerve and

C
R
A
S
H

INTO THE DITCH!

Evenings
and After Dark

Fi! Fo! Fum! Fee!
I sniff a big plate of chips for my tea.
Be they with fishball or burger or egg
I'll pour on the ketchup till everything's red.

What are little boys made of,
What are little boys made of?
Bearhugs, banged shins
And ragamuffin grins,
That's what little boys are made of.

What are little girls made of,
What are little girls made of?
Grazed knees and wriggles,
And freckledy giggles,
That's what little girls are made of.

BATHTIME

Bathtime is washy
And splashy
And wet.
I've scrubbed *both* my knees
And wiped round my neck.
Bathtime is lovely
And bubbly
And clean.
My toes are inspected
And fit to be seen.
Oh…
Don't you believe me?
That's *really* unfair.
I can't see my ears
'Cos they're covered by hair.

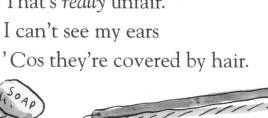

I'm a little parcel
trying
not
to
w
r
i
g
g
l
e
Wrap me in a towel
And poke me in the middle.
Will I be an ostrich?
Will I be a bee?
Will I be a crocodile?
Take me out and see!

Rub a dub dub,
Three babes in a tub
And who do you think got wet?
The daddy, the mummy,
The teddy bear's tummy,
So

Hoppity

Out

You

GET!

49

O My Grand Old Grandpa York
He had ten thousand teds,
He marched them into their baths every night,
Then he marched them to their beds.
And when they got in they were wet,
And when they got out they were dry,
And when they were all snuggled up very tight
He sang them a lullaby.

STORYTIME

Three little piglets lived up in a tree
One big and one small and one thinny-thin-thin
It was draughty and drippy and shiver-de-dee.
By the hairs on my snout and my chinny-chin-chin.

So Piggy Big moved to a house made of straw
One big and one small and one thinny-thin-thin
But bad Mr Wolf came and tapped at her door.
By the hairs on my snout and my chinny-chin-chin.

"Let me in, Piggy Big!" Said Big Piggy, "No! No!"
One big and one small and one thinny-thin-thin
So Wolf chuffed and snuffed and he started to blow.
By the hairs on my snout and my chinny-chin-chin.

The straw blew away. Piggy Big cried, "Wee wee!"
One big and one small and one thinny-thin-thin
And ran to her sisters safe up in the tree.
By the hairs on my snout and my chinny-chin-chin.

Piggy Small moved away to a house made of sticks
One big and one small and one thinny-thin-thin
When Wolf tiptoed up a lick-licking his lips.
By the hairs on my snout and my chinny-chin-chin.

"Let me in, Piggy Small!" Said Small Piggy, "No! No!"
One big and one small and one thinny-thin-thin
So Wolf took a deep breath and started to blow.
By the hairs on my snout and my chinny-chin-chin.

The sticks blew away, Piggy Small cried, "Wee wee!"
One big and one small and one thinny-thin-thin
And ran to her sisters safe up in the tree.
By the hairs on my snout and my chinny-chin-chin.

Piggy Thin moved away to a house made of stone
One big and one small and one thinny-thin-thin
So Wolf called her up on his portable phone.
By the hairs on my snout and my chinny-chin-chin.

"Let me in, Piggy Thin!" Said Thin Piggy "No! NO!"
One big and one small and one thinny-thin-thin
So Wolf puffed his cheeks out and started to blow.
By the hairs on my snout and my chinny-chin chin.

He blew at the window, he blew at the lock
One big and one small and one thinny-thin-thin
The house stayed as steady as mountains of rock.
By the hairs on my snout and my chinny-chin-chin.

Wolf huffed till his tail hairs turned all roundabout
One big and one small and one thinny-thin-thin
He huffed himself backwards and near inside-out.
By the hairs on my snout and my chinny-chin-chin.

But Piggy Thin's house stood as firm as a hill
One big and one small and one thinny-thin-thin
And all three pig sisters are living there still.
By the hairs on my snout and my chinny-chin-chin.

Poor Wolf slunk off home to his cubs and his mate
One big and one small and one thinny-thin-thin
They had no pork supper, just six empty plates.
By the hairs on my snout and my chinny-chin-chin

empty plate with
no pork dinner on.

Young Prince Cole
Was a mischievous soul,
And a mischievous soul was he.
He hid the king's pipe
And he broke the king's bowl,
And he chased the royal fiddlers three.
"Tootle tootle too," sang the trumpets,
"Rumble tumble tum," growled the drums,
"Grumble grumble grum," cried the king, very crossly,
"Bring that naughty boy back to me,
Back to me, to me, to me."

Young Prince Cole
Was a mischievous soul,
And a mischievous soul was he.
He stuck out his tongue
And he tripped up the queen,
And he laughed at the fiddlers three.
"Tootle tootle too," sang the trumpets,
"Rumble tumble tum" growled the drums,
"Grumble grumble grum" cried the king, very crossly,
"Bring that wretched boy back to me,
Back to me, to me, to me."

Young Prince Cole
Was a mischievous soul,
And a mischievous soul was he.
He emptied the moat
And he threw in the cat,
And he kicked all the fiddlers three.
"Tootle tootle too," sang the trumpets,
"Rumble tumble tum," growled the drums,
"Grumble grumble grum" cried the king, very crossly,
"Bring that dreadful boy back to me,
Back to me, to me, to me."

Young Prince Cole
Was a mischievous soul,
And a mischievous soul was he.
He ran extremely fast
But they caught him at last,
Those furious fiddlers three.
"Tootle tootle too," sang the trumpets,
"Rumble tumble tum," growled the drums,
"Grumble grumble grum," cried the king, when he saw him,
"You shall go without the royal tea.
Royal tea, royal tea tea tea tea tea."

A boy sold a cow,
A boy called Jack.
He sold her for beans
In an old velvet hat.

They planted the beans,
And watched them grow.
One, two, three,
And away they go!

Jack trotted home,
— No money, no cow —
What will poor Jack
And his mother eat now?

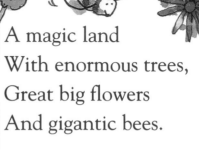

Up through the clouds,
Up to the sky,
A leafy green ladder,
Higher than high.

Up climbed Jack,
Hand over hand,
Till his head popped out
In another land.

A magic land
With enormous trees,
Great big flowers
And gigantic bees.

A huge green castle
With golden doors,
Diamond windows,
And marble floors.

side door   front door   other side door

In went Jack
As brave as a flea,
Tiptoed inside,
What did he see?

A horrible giant
With a purple nose,
Haystack hair,
And fifteen toes.

The giant was snoring
Like ninety-nine trains,
Like forty-one diggers
Or ten creaky cranes.

A harp and a hen
Lay down by his feet.
Yum yummy thought Jack,
Roast chicken to eat!

Jack stole a bag,
He opened it wide,
He stuffed both the hen
And the harp inside.

Jack ran out
As quick as he could.
He ran through the flowers
And the bees and the wood.

But the hen woke up
And pecked at a string.
The harp gave a trill
As it started to sing.

Stop thief, stop thief!
Master, Master!
Jack shut the bag tight,
And ran even faster.

Fee roared the giant,
Fee, fi, fo, fum!
I taste the blood of a thief
On my tongue.

Tender young thief,
With carrots and rice,
And a strong cheese sauce
Would be very nice.

The beanstalk shuddered
Above Jack's head,
The branches shook
At the giant's tread.

Jack took his axe,
Went CHOP CHOP CHOP
He chopped till the beanstalk
Began to drop.

The giant fell down
With a CRASH CRASH CRASH!
His neck and his bones
Broke SMASH SMASH SMASH!

Jack picked up the bag
Which he'd flung to the ground,
He opened it up,
And look what he found!

gold
egg

A hen and a harp
With magical power,
The hen laid an egg
Made of gold, every hour.

wondrous song
being played by
magic Harp

The harp granted wishes,
And played wondrous songs,
So Jack and his mother
Danced all the day long.

very big presents for
all their friends –
especially Me!!

They lived all their lives
Full of loving and laughter,
And gave their friends presents
For ever and after.

the
End

BEDTIME

Rock-a-bye-baby
What do you see?
Leaves in the greenwood,
Ships on the sea.
Moon rides the night sky,
Sun sails the West,
So hush, little baby,
Sleep now, and rest.

Nighty night,
Sleepy tight,
Don't let those buggies bite.
If they bite
(And some of them do)
Smack their behinds
With the sole of your shoe.

Twinkle, twinkle, little star,
Shining down from lands afar.
Like a tiny guiding light
In the deserts of the night.
Twinkle, twinkle, little star,
Shine on me from lands afar.

Cushlamochree, O Cushlamochree,
Shall you dance for the stars?
Shall you play with the sea?
Shall you swim like the whale?
Shall you follow the sun?
O Cushlamochree, has your dreaming begun?

Cariad Bach, O Cariad Bach
Shall you sing to the moon?
Shall you shout for the dark?
Shall you whisper with bears?
Shall you waken the night?
O Cariad Bach, soft dreams and sleep tight.

Cushlamochree is Gaelic for darling
Cariad Bach is Welsh for little darling